EARTH CYCLES

PLANT LIFE CYCLES

by Sally Morgan

A+

Smart Apple Media

Published by Smart Apple Media
P.O. Box 3263, Mankato, Minnesota 56002

Printed in the United States of America at Corporate Graphics, in North Mankato, Minnesota.

Published by arrangement with the Watts Publishing Group Ltd., London.

Library of Congress Cataloging-in-Publication Data
Morgan, Sally, 1957-
  Plant life cycles / by Sally Morgan.
       p. cm. -- (Earth cycles)
  Summary: "Discusses the different species of plants and their life cycles.
  Also introduces how insects, birds, and nature help in pollination and
  the role plants play in food chains. Includes diagrams"--Provided by publisher.
  Includes bibliographical references and index.
  ISBN 978-1-59920-524-3 (library binding : alk. paper)
  1. Plants--Juvenile literature. 2. Plant life cycles--Juvenile literature. I. Title. II. Series: Morgan, Sally, 1957-.
Earth cycles.
  QK49.M8564 2012
  580--dc22

                                    2010030420

Produced for Franklin Watts by
White-Thomson Publishing, Ltd.
Editor: Jean Coppendale
Design: Paul Manning

Picture credits
t = top b = bottom l = left = r = right
1, ECO/Paul Thompson; 3, 16b, ECO/Robert Pickett; 3, 31, Shutterstock/Marty Kropp; 4r, Shutterstock/Dole; 4bl,
ECO/Richard Glover; 5b, Shutterstock/Ultrashock; 5r, ECO/Chinch Gryniewicz; 6t, Shutterstock/Martin
Muránsky; 6b, ECO/Phillip Colla; 7t, ECO/Sally Morgan; 7b, ECO/Genevieve Leaper; 7r, ECO/Sally Morgan; 8l,9b
Shutterstock/Stephen Coburn; 8 (seed case), Shutterstock/Nikolay Okhitin; 8 (shoot), ECO/Robert Pickett; 8
(sunflower withering), ECO/Robert Pickett; 9 (sunflower before flowering), ECO/Robert Pickett; 9 (sunflower
bud), Shutterstock/Joy Brown; 9 (bamboo), Shutterstock/Zhu Difeng; 10bl, Shutterstock/Lepas; 10 (seed case 1-4),
ECO/Sally Morgan; 11bl, ECO/Wayne Lawler; 11r, ECO/Christine Osborne; 12t, ECO/Frank Blackburn; 12b,
Shutterstock/Jovan Nikolic; 13b, Shutterstock/Petr Jilek; 13r, Bluemoose images; 14t, Shutterstock/David Dea; 14b,
ECO/Vicki Coombs; 15r, ECO/David Wootton Photography; 15l, ECO/Peter Cairns; 16t, Shutterstock/Ariel Bravy;
17l, ECO/Robert Pickett; 18r, Shutterstock/Andreas Gradin; 18l, Shutterstock/Anette Linnea Rasmussen; 19t,
ECO/Fritz Polking; 19b, Shutterstock/Vaide Seskauskiene; 19t, Shutterstock/Lim Yong Hian; 20b, Shutterstock/Scott
Leman; 20t, Shutterstock/Graeme Dawes; 21l, Shutterstock/Patrizia Tilly; 21r, Shutterstock/Julie Lucht; 22t,
Shutterstock/Vitezslav Halamka; 22, ECO/Sally Morgan; 23r, Shutterstock/Christopher Elwell; 24, ECO/Fritz
Polking; 25l, ECO/Reinhard Dirscherl; 25r, ECO/Robert Pickett; 26, Shutterstock/Anton Foltin; 27l,
Shutterstock/newphotoservice; 27r, ECO/Chinch Gryniewicz; 28b, Shutterstock/Christopher Elwell; 28 (background
image), ECO/Andrew Brown; 28t, ECO/Simon Grove; 29, ECO/Kevin King.

Note to parents and teachers
Every effort has been made by the publishers to ensure that the web sites listed on page 32 are suitable for children,
that they are of the highest educational value, and that they contain no inappropriate or offensive material.
However, because of the nature of the Internet, it is impossible to guarantee that the contents of these sites have
not be altered. We strongly advise that Internet access is supervised by a responsible adult.

1018
3-2011

9 8 7 6 5 4 3 2 1

Contents

Words appearing in **bold** like this can be found in the glossary on pages 30–31.

What Is a Plant?

Plants are living **organisms** that make their own food, grow, and **reproduce**. They come in all sizes, from tiny plants floating in the oceans to huge trees growing in woods and forests.

Shoots

A typical plant is made up of a shoot and root. The shoot is the part of the plant that grows above the ground. It consists of stems and leaves. In large plants, such as trees, the stem is thick and woody and is called a trunk. Plant leaves are usually green, and they make the food the plant needs by using sunlight.

leaf

shoot

stem

► This plant has grown from a seed. The shoot consists of the stem and the leaves.

remains of seed

root

► Green leaves trap light energy from the sun and use it to make food.

Roots

Roots grow underground. They anchor, or hold, the plant in place and take in water and **minerals** from the soil. Plants have different types of roots. For example, some vegetables, such as carrots, have tap roots that are large and thick. Other plants, such as geraniums, have **fibrous roots** that are thin and thread-like.

Life Cycle

Some plants produce flowers, and the flowers produce **seeds**. In this book, you will learn about all the different stages that make up the **life cycle** of a plant.

Q What tree is nicknamed the upside-down tree?

A The baobab. This tree is found in Africa, Madagascar, and Australia. In the dry season, it drops all its leaves, and its branches look like roots. The tree stores water in its huge trunk so that it can survive long periods without rain.

▼ This is the brightly colored flower of the bird-of-paradise plant.

▲ Baobab tree

5

All Types of Plants

There are more than 375,000 different **species**, or types, of plants. To make it easier to identify plants, scientists have divided them into different groups. This is called **classification**. All the plants in the same group have features in common. For example, all mosses lack a **root system**.

▼ The hibiscus is a type of flowering plant.

Flowering Plants

The largest group of plants is the flowering plants with about 250,000 species. All these plants produce flowers. Examples are daisies, sunflowers, and apple trees.

Nonflowering Plants

All the other plants are nonflowering plants. They include the **algae**, mosses, ferns, and **conifers**. The simplest plants are algae, such as seaweeds. Algae do not have roots and leaves, and most live in water.

◄ Kelp is a type of seaweed. It is found in shallow water and its **fronds** can grow up to 16 inches (40 cm) a day.

Clumps of moss can be found growing on walls.

Q and A

Q What is the world's largest plant?

A The giant sequoia or redwood tree. This is a type of conifer found in California. One particular tree, nicknamed General Sherman, is the tallest in the world. It is 275 feet (84 m) tall and more than 2,000 years old. Its trunk weighs about 2,200 tons (2,000 t) —that's more than 400 elephants!

Mosses are small, simple plants that grow in damp, shady places. Their oval leaves are arranged in a spiral around the stem. They are anchored in the ground by short threads that take in water from the air.

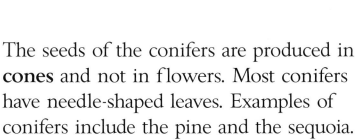

▲ The leaf of the fern is called a frond. The small leaves that make up the frond are called pinnae.

▲ Giant sequoia

The seeds of the conifers are produced in **cones** and not in flowers. Most conifers have needle-shaped leaves. Examples of conifers include the pine and the sequoia.

Life of a Plant

A plant goes through several changes as it grows.

Flowering plants start life as a seed. The seed starts to **germinate**, or sprout, and becomes a seedling. This gets larger and grows into an adult plant that produces flowers. The flower then produces seeds that grow into new plants.

2
A shoot grows above the ground and new leaves appear.

seed coat

new root

seeds

1
The seed germinates. Roots grow down into the soil.

▲ This shows the life cycle of a sunflower. It is an annual plant—it germinates, flowers, and dies in one year.

6
The petals fall away and the seeds form. The seeds drop to the ground, and the shoot withers and dies.

Q What is the world's fastest-growing plant?

A The bamboo. This fast-growing tropical grass grows so fast that you can almost watch it grow! Most bamboo grows 4–6 inches (10–15 cm) a day. But scientists have recorded the stem of some bamboo plants growing at just over 47 inches (120 cm) in a single day.

3

The shoot grows taller and more leaves form.

bud

petals

4

A bud forms at the top of the shoot.

▲ Bamboo

5

The petals open. The bright color attracts insects.

9

Seeds and Germination

The life cycle of a flowering plant starts with the seed.

A seed contains an **embryo**, which is a tiny plant. Around the seed is a protective coat, and a store of food is found inside.

Starting to Grow

The first stage is to take in water. This causes the seed to swell and the seed coat splits. The food stored inside the seed is used to help it grow. Soon, the first root appears. It grows down into the soil to anchor the seed in place. Then the shoot pushes up above the soil.

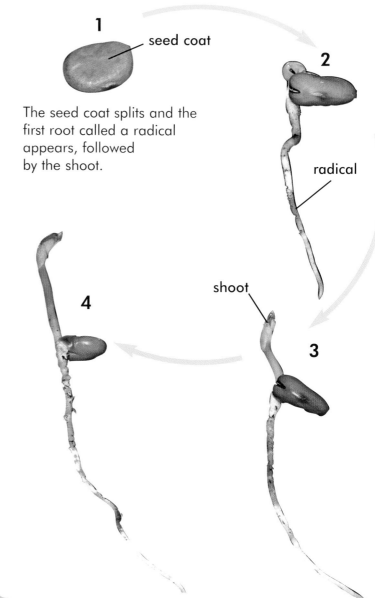

1 seed coat

The seed coat splits and the first root called a radical appears, followed by the shoot.

2 radical

3 shoot

4

▲ Pea seeds are packed with food that the embryos need to germinate.

When to Germinate

Seeds need the right conditions to start germinating. All seeds need water and air. Some germinate only when the temperature is right, so they may need warmth or cold. A few seeds, such as the lettuce seed, need light.

Tree Seeds

The seeds of many tree species need to experience freezing conditions before they germinate. This stops them from growing in fall instead of spring. Some seeds have a really tough seed coat and they only germinate when the seed has been damaged. For example, the seeds of the yew and juniper trees germinate after an animal eats them. The seed coat is damaged as the seed passes through the animal's body.

Special Needs

Some seeds need unusual conditions to germinate. Banksia plants are evergreen shrubs and trees found in Australia. They are killed by fires, but their seeds survive and germinate after the fire. The trigger for these seeds to germinate is smoke.

Q Can old seeds still germinate?

A Yes. In 1973, seeds of the date palm were found in an **archaeological site** at King Herod's temple in Masada in the Middle East. These seeds were 2,000 years old. In 2005, a scientist successfully germinated one of them.

▲ Date palm

▶ This is a seed head of the banksia plant. The seeds will remain in the seed pod until released by a fire. Then they will start to grow.

Making Food

Plants have green leaves. This is because the leaves are packed with a green substance called **chlorophyll**. The plant uses the chlorophyll to make food in a process called **photosynthesis**.

Photosynthesis

A plant needs light energy from the sun, **carbon dioxide** from the air, and water from the soil to photosynthesize. The light energy is trapped by the chlorophyll and is used to combine the carbon dioxide and the water to make sugar. The plant uses the sugar as a fuel for growth.

▲ Most leaves are broad and thin so that they can trap as much light as possible.

▼ Excess sugar is changed to starch and stored in the roots of these parsnips.

From Sugar to Protein

Some sugar is used by the leaves to help them grow and to make other substances such as **protein**. The rest is transported around the plant in tubes. These tubes run through the stem and ensure that the sugar goes where it is needed, for example, to the growing tips of the shoot. Excess sugar is stored in the roots and other storage organs.

Q and A

Oxygen

Oxygen is also produced by photosynthesis. Both plants and animals need oxygen for **respiration**. This is the process that breaks down foods, such as sugar. Any oxygen not needed by the plant moves out into the air through the plant's leaves. Oxygen in the air is taken up by animals.

Plants need minerals such as **potassium** and **magnesium** for healthy growth. These minerals are taken in from the soil by the roots.

Q Which leaves close when they are touched?

A The leaves of the sensitive plant, also known as "touch-me-not." When you touch the leaf of this plant, it immediately closes and drops down, and then some of the other leaves close. It slowly opens its leaves again after about 30 minutes. This reaction may protect the plant from grazing animals.

closed leaf

◀ The roots of this tree have grown down through the soil. They anchor the tree in the ground and also take in water and minerals.

▲ Sensitive plant

Flowers

Flowers are vital in the life cycle of the flowering plant because they are involved in reproduction.

Flower Structure

A typical flower has petals that surround the reproductive organs. The male reproductive part is called the stamen, which is made up of an **anther** and a stalk called the **filament**. The anther produces yellow dust-like grains of **pollen**. The female part is the **pistil**, and it is made up of the **stigma**, **style**, and **ovary**. Inside the ovary is the **ovule**, which contains the egg.

▲ The flower of the thistle is made up of many small flowers grouped together. They form a single, large flower head.

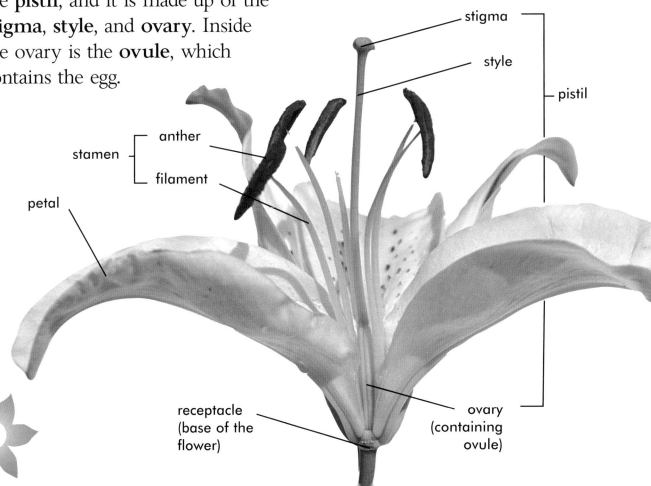

stigma

style

pistil

stamen

anther

filament

petal

receptacle (base of the flower)

ovary (containing ovule)

Pollination

Plant reproduction starts with **pollination**. This is the transfer of pollen from the anther to the stigma. Some flowers pollinate themselves as the pollen drops off the anther straight on to the stigma. Others need animals, such as insects, to carry the pollen from one flower to another. There are also wind-pollinated flowers, where the wind carries the pollen to the stigma.

Q What is the world's largest flower?

A Rafflesia. This is the flower of a **vine** that is found underground in the rain forests of Southeast Asia. Only the flower appears above ground. The flower can reach a diameter of 40 in. (100 cm) and may weigh up to 22 lbs. (10 kg). It is also very smelly to attract flies!

▲ Cotton grass, named after its cotton-like seed heads, is a wind-pollinated plant.

Fertilization

Once pollination has taken place, the pollen grain produces a long tube that grows down through the style to the ovule. There, it joins with the egg. This is called **fertilization** and it produces an embryo.

▲ Rafflesia

15

Flowers and Insects

Insect-pollinated flowers need to attract insects—so they advertise!

Bright Colors

Most flowers that are pollinated by insects are brightly colored. This makes them easy to see and attracts bees and other insects. Some plants also have **nectar**, a sweet juice that insects love. As the insects drink the nectar, they pollinate the flower.

▲ The bee crawls right inside the flower of this foxglove to reach the nectar. As it does so, the pollen drops onto its hairy back.

Flower Shapes

To help insects pollinate them easily, flowers are different shapes. The foxglove is shaped like a bell so bees can crawl in. Sunflowers, thistles, and daisies have open flowers with short anthers. Insects pick up the pollen as they crawl over the flower.

▶ The butterfly's legs become covered in pollen as it climbs over the flower. It carries the pollen to other flowers.

16

Flower Trickery

Some plants have flowers that trick insects into pollinating them. The flowers look like female insects and have a scent that attracts male insects. When male bees try to mate with the flower, they pick up pollen, which they then carry to the next plant. Some orchids are named after the inscct their flower looks like, such as the bee, spider, and fly orchids.

Q What is the world's smelliest flower?

A The titan arum. Its flower produces a stench like rotting flesh that attracts swarms of flies. They crawl all over it and even lay their eggs on the petals. The flies carry the pollen to the stigmas so the flower can make seeds. The smell of the flower is so strong that it can be detected from 1,100 yards (1 km) away!

▲ The flowers of the bee orchid look just like a large bumblebee.

▲ Titan arum

Seeds and Fruits

Once a flower has been pollinated and fertilized, its petals drop off. The ovary swells and becomes a fruit while the ovule becomes the seed.

All Sorts of Fruits

Most people think of fruits as being sweet tasting. For example, we eat the soft, sweet flesh of fruits such as plums and peaches but not the hard pit, or seed, in the center. The fruit of the pea and bean is the pod. The pod swells up around the seeds (the peas and beans) and protects them. We don't eat the pod, but we eat the seeds inside.

▲ The sycamore produces a winged fruit. Part of the fruit extends to form a thin, dry wing.

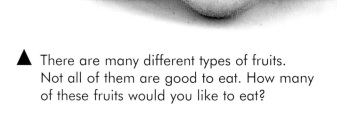

▲ There are many different types of fruits. Not all of them are good to eat. How many of these fruits would you like to eat?

The cones found on pine trees are fruits.

Q What is the world's smelliest fruit?

A The durian. The fruit is green and spiky with a very strong smell. Some people like it, but others find it disgusting. However, the powerful smell attracts animals from afar, and they come to pick up the fruit and help disperse the seeds.

False Fruits

Not all fruits are true fruits. In some plants, the base, or **receptacle**, of the flower swells up to form a fruit-like structure. For example, many people think of the strawberry as a fruit, but the fruits are actually the tiny specks on the outside.

▼ These rose hips are the fruits of roses. They have developed from the base of the flowers.

▲ Durian

19

Scattering Seeds

Seeds have to be scattered to prevent the seedlings from germinating near the parent plant where they would have to compete for light and water.

Flung Out

The pods of peas and beans become drier as they ripen. Eventually, they split, flinging out the seeds far away from the parent plant.

tiny holes here allow seeds to escape in the wind

▲ The seed head of the poppy dries out and small holes form to allow the seeds to be flung out.

◄ These two rainbow lorikeets from Australia are eating an apple.

Eaten by Animals

Tasty fruits are picked up and eaten by animals. The seeds pass through the animal's body and are left on the ground in its droppings, far away from the parent plant.

Gliders

Some seeds have wings or parachutes so they catch the wind and land away from the parent plant. Gliders are seeds with papery wings that spiral slowly to the ground. Plants such as dandelions, goat's beard, and milkweed produce seeds with a tuft of hairs a bit like a parachute. The parachute catches the wind and the seed is carried long distances, even over mountains.

Q What seeds are hitchhikers?

A Burs, the seed of the burdock. These seeds have hooks, which become attached to the fur of any animal that brushes up against the seed head. The Swiss inventor George de Mestral came up with the idea of the fabric fastening material called Velcro from finding burs in the fur of his dog.

parachute

▲ Dandelion seeds have a small parachute and they are carried away on the wind.

▲ Burdock

Carried by Water

Some seeds are carried by water. For example, the coconut, the seed of the palm tree, is often seen growing on beaches. The coconut floats in water so it is carried away by the tides to other beaches where the seed germinates.

Bulbs, Runners, and Tubers

Some plants can reproduce without producing seeds. They produce **bulbs**, **runners**, or **tubers** that grow into new plants. This is called **asexual reproduction**.

Bulbs

Daffodils, tulips, and onions all produce bulbs. A bulb is a swollen structure that forms at the bottom of the stem, just below ground level. It is filled with food. The bulb remains underground over winter, and in spring, the stored food is used to grow new leaves. Many smaller bulbs form around the main bulb.

▲ The onion bulb forms in summer at the base of the leaves.

Runners

A strawberry plant produces a long stem called a runner that grows over the ground. New plants form where the runner touches the soil. The new plants are identical to the parent plant.

▶ A single strawberry plant can produce many new plants each year.

runner

Tubers

Potatoes are plants that multiply by producing tubers. A tuber is a swelling on an underground stem. During the summer, the plant sends all its spare sugar to the tubers in the ground. There, the sugar is changed into **starch** and stored. The plant dies in fall but the tubers survive, and in spring, they start to sprout. They use the starch as a source of food.

Q What is a cutting?

A A cutting is a short length of stem with a leaf that, if treated correctly, can grow into a new plant. Gardeners take cuttings of their plants to grow new plants. If you place a cutting of a plant, such as a geranium, in water, it will grow roots within a couple of weeks.

▼ Each tuber can grow into a new plant, so one potato plant becomes many new potato plants.

tubers

Food Chains

A **food chain** shows the feeding relationships between the plants and animals that share the same habitat.

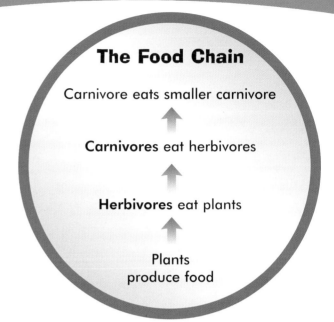

The Food Chain

Carnivore eats smaller carnivore

↑

Carnivores eat herbivores

↑

Herbivores eat plants

↑

Plants
produce food

▲ Herbivores, such as this black rhino, are adapted to eating plants. It eats the leaves of trees and shrubs, such as this acacia plant.

Producers and Consumers

Plants are **producers** because they make their own food. They are at the start, or bottom, of the food chain. Animals cannot make their own food, so they eat plants or other animals. Plant-eating animals are called herbivores. They have large, ridged teeth so they can chew grass, and their **gut** can break down tough plant foods.

Meat-eating animals, called carnivores, eat other animals. Sometimes, a carnivore is eaten by another carnivore. For example, worms are eaten by blackbirds and blackbirds may be eaten by birds of prey. The last animal in the food chain is the top carnivore. Lions are an example of a top carnivore.

Ocean Chains

There are food chains in the oceans, too. The producers are the seaweeds and tiny plant **plankton** that float in the sea. The plant plankton is eaten by animal plankton, which in turn is eaten by small fish. The small fish are eaten by larger fish or mammals such as dolphins.

▼ A whale shark is the biggest fish in the ocean, but it feeds on plankton.

Q Which animals can completely destroy a field of crops in a few hours?

A A swarm of locusts. A locust plague may contain billions of these insects. Each locust eats the equivalent of its body mass each day. Imagine how much a billion locusts could eat in a day!

▲ Locust

How Long Do Plants Live?

Some plants live for only a few months. Most live for many years and a few live for thousands of years.

Plants can be divided into three groups according to how long they live. These are annuals, biennials, and perennials.

Annuals

Annuals are plants that live for only one year. They grow quickly and produce flowers and lots of seeds. Then they die. Annuals include meadow plants such as poppies, corncockles, and cornflowers.

▼ After rains fall in the desert, the seeds of annual plants such as poppies germinate. Soon there is a mass of flowers across the desert.

Q and A

Biennials

Biennials live for two years. The seeds germinate in summer and grow through winter. They produce their flowers and seeds during the second summer and then die. Biennials include foxgloves and globe artichokes.

Q What is the oldest plant?

A The King's holly. This low-growing shrub was discovered growing in a remote rain forest in Tasmania, Australia. It may be more than 43,000 years old!

Perennials

Perennials live for many years. The shoots of perennials die off in fall and reappear the following spring. Perennials that have woody stems, such as trees and shrubs, do not die off. Perennials also include garden plants such as peonies.

▲ **Herbaceous plants** have non-woody stems. The yarrow (yellow) and phlox (pink) in this garden grow all through the summer before dying off in fall and reappearing in spring.

Recycling Plants

Dead plants are eaten by organisms called **decomposers**. If this did not happen, the ground would be covered in piles of dead leaves!

Decaying Leaves

When a leaf lands on the ground, it may be eaten by animals such as earthworms and beetles. Small decomposers, such as **bacteria** and **fungi**, also feed on the remains. Over time, the leaf slowly disappears. The valuable **nutrients** go into the soil where they can be taken in by plant roots and used for growth.

▲ The soft parts of a leaf are the first to decay. The tougher veins take much longer to break down.

► Mushrooms, a type of fungi, are found growing on rotting logs and dead leaves.

Q and A

Compost Piles

Gardeners get rid of dead leaves and weeds in a **compost** pile. They pile up the waste and wait for the decomposers to get to work. The decomposers release heat as they break down the remains and this warms up the inside of the compost pile. The heat is useful as it speeds up the whole process. After a year or so, the plant remains have been broken down and a soil-like compost has formed. This is rich in nutrients, so it can be put on the soil to help plants grow.

Q How long does a leaf take to decay?

A It can take less than six months for a fallen leaf to be recycled in a rain forest. This is because of the high temperatures and moisture. In cooler forests, leaves may lie on the ground for years before they are completely broken down.

▼ These leaves will break down to form compost that can be spread on the soil.

compost

29

Glossary

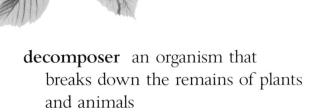

algae simple plants that are found in water and in damp places

anther male part of the plant that produces pollen

archaeological site an area set aside for studying people who lived long ago

asexual reproduction reproduction that does not involve seeds, for example when plants reproduce by producing tubers or runners

bacteria microscopic organism consisting of a single cell; some are helpful, but others cause disease.

bulb an underground storage organ formed from the swollen bases of leaves; an onion is a bulb.

carbon dioxide a colorless gas found in air

chlorophyll the green pigment in plants used in photosynthesis

classification the process of dividing organisms into different groups according to their features

compost a rich soil formed from decayed plants and other organic matter

cone the fruit of a conifer that contains the seeds

conifer a tree that has needle-shaped leaves and produces cones rather than flowers

decomposer an organism that breaks down the remains of plants and animals

embryo an organism in its earliest stage of development

fertilization the joining together of the male cell in pollen with the egg in the ovule

fibrous roots fine, branched roots that form a network in the soil

filament a thin stalk that holds up the anther, or male part, of a plant

food chain a series of organisms in a community of which each member feeds on another in the chain

frond the leaf-like part of a seaweed or fern

fungi a simple organism that lacks chlorophyll, such as a mushroom, mold, and mildew

germinate start to grow; to sprout from a seed

gut a long tube running through the body where food is digested

herbaceous plant a plant that dics off in fall, spends winter in the ground, and grows again the following spring

life cycle a series of changes that an organism undergoes from birth to death

magnesium essential nutrient needed by plants to make chlorophyll

minerals nutrients found in the soil

nectar sugary liquid produced by flowers

nutrients the minerals needed for healthy growth

organism a living thing

ovary part of the pistil; the female reproductive part of a flower

ovule the structure in the pistil that contains the egg and develops into a seed after fertilization

photosynthesis making food using light; the process by which plants make their food

pistil the female part of a flower which is made up of the stigma, style, and ovary

plankton tiny plants and animals floating near the surface in water

pollen tiny yellow particles produced by the anthers

pollination the transfer of pollen to the stigma of the pistil

potassium essential nutrient plants need for healthy growth

producer organism that produces its own food, for example a plant

protein an important substance that a plant uses for growth and repair

receptacle the bottom part of a flower to which the petals, stamens, and pistils are attached

reproduce to produce offspring or new plants

respiration a process that uses oxygen to break down food to release energy; carbon dioxide is a waste product.

root system all the roots of a plant or all the underground parts of a plant

runner a long stem that grows along the ground

seed a structure that contains a plant embryo; formed from the ovule

species a group of organisms with the same features that can breed with each other

starch an energy-rich substance made by plants

stigma the sticky end of the pistil on which the pollen lands

style part of the pistil that links the stigma to the ovary

tuber a storage organ that forms on underground stems; potatoes are tubers.

vine a climbing plant, for example a grape vine

Further Reading

Blashfield, Jean F. *Plant Life.* Gareth Stevens Pub., 2007.

Brown, Harriet. *Food from the Sun: How Plants Live and Grow.* Rourke Pub., 2008.

Llewellyn, Claire. *The Life of Plants.* Smart Apple Media, 2008.

Morgan, Sally. *The Plant Cycle.* PowerKids Press, 2009.

Web Sites

Gardening with Children
www.bbc.co.uk/gardening/gardening_with_children
The whole family can enjoy gardening with activities from this web site.

The Great Plant Escape
www.urbanext.uiuc.edu/gpe
Help Detective Leplant and his partners Bud and Sprout unlock the mysteries of plant life.

The Life Cycle of Plants
http://www2.bgfl.org/bgfl2/custom/resources_ftp/client_ftp/ks2/science/plants_pt2
Learn about the plant life cycle with this interactive site.

Index